AIR PLANTS:

STEP BY STEP GUIDE TO GROWING TILLANDSIA + TIPS FOR INDOOR PLANTS

GEORGE BEST

CHAPTER ONE   6

PRELUDE TO AIR PLANTS   6

WHY YOU NEED AIR PLANTS   11

CHAPTER TWO CLASSIFICATION OF AIR PLANT   20

AIR PLANTS GROWTH PHASES   68

MAKING AIR PLANT BLOOM FAST   70

AIR PLANT SHOPPING   79

WHAT NEXT AFTER YOUR AIR PLANT ARRIVED   81

CHAPTER THREE   83

PERFECT AIR PLANT ENVIRONMENT   83

CHAPTER FOUR   90

AIR PLANT FEEDING   90

BLOOMING PHASE WATERING   94

CARE AND MAINTENANCE OF AIR PLANT   98

REVIVING A DYING OR SICK AIR PLANT   106

CHAPTER FIVE   110

DISPLAYING AND MOUNTING AIR PLANT   110

AIR PLANTS TRIMMING   122

HOW TO DIVIDE AIR PLANTS   126

CHAPTER SIX   129

AIR PLANT PEST AND DISEASES   129

CHAPTER SEVEN   139

AIR PLANT GARDENING TOOLS   139

CHAPTER ONE

PRELUDE TO AIR PLANTS

Tillandsia plants are indigenous to the temperate region of South and Central America and even North America. They are plants that belong to the Bromeliad family. They can survive well in arid areas like deserts, mountains, and rainforest. Essentially, air plants are epiphyte because they do not need soil to thrive. They get their nutrients from air, water and they grow roots that allow the plant to use the roots to attach themselves to mountains, rocks, trees, among others. They need the root for only one purpose which is for support only and not for the purpose of using the roots to obtain nutrients. Where air plant becomes too long due to excessive growth, you can trim them back to size with a scissor.

In the wild, air plants are known to cling to rocky surfaces and on the surfaces of trees. There are over 500 varieties of Tillandsia that grow in different habitats. Tillandsia grows especially in the wild on high altitude mostly mountainous terrain, steamy jungles, arid desserts, a cloudy forest that is cool and high mountain ridges. The bromeliads family is very diverse indeed and they are found mainly in the tropical and subtropical areas. The factor that helps these plants to grow in a difficult environment is their trichome. A trichome is an outgrowth of a plant's outer cell layer that is called the epidermis. Most plants have trichome but in the bromeliad family, especially Tillandsia, they have developed their own in a very advanced manner and fashion. The trichome in some ways influences the appearance of Tillandsia. Due to the presence of trichome, some of them have silver and white appearance. These unique organs found in Tillandsia enable them to be an expert in nutrient scavenging. It is interesting to know that while many plants obtain their nutrients from the soil using well-built root hair. Tillandsia on the other hand, taps their nutrients from a unique source. They get their nutrients from rain water, leaf debris, fog, and dust.

Though air plants can survive and thrive on little nutrients compared to other plants, however, it does not mean that they should not be well fed with the adequate nutrient source. Their feeding can be a couple of times in a week while other nutrients such as fertilizer can be used to feed the plant once in a month. Since these plants do not live in the soil like other contemporary plants, they cannot break down urea nitrogen. It is important to get a fertilizer that is not urea based. If you look at your fertilizer details, you will see NPK. The N means that it has nitrogen contained in it. However, an NPK fertilizer with 20 -10 – 20, 20 – 20 – 20 can be used for your plants. Your plant can be fed with a non-urea fertilizer for at least once in a month.

These plants need water to thrive. They must be fed with the best type of water that is available for their growth. For the best type of water for your air plant, it is essentially important for you to use rainwater if it is available to you or tap water which must be left for minimum 12 hours to vaporize before usage. The details of what type of water to use for your air plant is covered in the small topic, best water for air plants. In cooler temperatures, the mesic green species needs more water than their silvery xeric family.

When it comes to lightening, air plant loves indirect sunlight or artificial light. If the plants are indoors, they also need sufficient light for their growth and bloom. For those air plants whose leaves looks green or are shiny, they require less light than the silver-colored air plant. If the green-leaf Tillandsia are exposed to too much sun, they can be sunburnt.

The area where the plant is must have some level of air circulation. You can use artificially generated air such as air from the fan for your plants.

When it comes to displaying your air plant, they can be mounted on a piece of wood or cork stone or any place that will allow them to attach themselves firmly. You can make use of a silver wire to attach them together. As they grow, they develop their own roots. They can be displayed either by hanging them or other methods of display.

Welcome to this air plant arena, sit down and enjoy the ride.

WHY YOU NEED AIR PLANTS

Air Purification

As a result of the special features that Tillandsia possess, your home will be free from chemical substances created from your air conditioner, electronic devices, cooking items, and the chemicals that are carried through your windows into your home.

Beyond the purification function which air plant do for your home, they also improve air quality. During photosynthesis, air plant improves air quality as they absorb carbon dioxide and convert it into oxygen which is what your body needs. A research by scientist established that indoor plants like Tillandsia eliminate chemical pollutants in the air and increase the amount of oxygen which gives you a very healthy office or home environment.

Minimal Maintenance Cost

There is no plant like Tillandsia when it comes to the cost of maintenance. It requires just a onetime purchase and no more. You do not need to replant them each year like you will have to do with other plants. Tillandsia's life cycle ensures that they produce their own babies known as pups. If they are properly taken care of, these pups will grow, passing each life phase, growth phase, blooming phase, pup phase and clumping phase. When they eventually reached maturity, they also produce their own babies and then the mother plant dies off. Which plant have you seen like this that have this kind of capacity? Well, this unique ability of reproduction gives air plant a special feature of maintenance with a little amount of dollars. You don't have to repurchase them for planting.

Environmental Beautification

The more relax, peaceful and beautiful the environment where you spend your resting time in the mornings, evenings and weekends the more you are able to manage stress that you have gathered in the course of the week activities. One benefit of having air plants in your home is that it can improve the interior appearance of your house. You can combine your Tillandsia with some objects in your home to give them a perfect outlook. Besides internal beautification, Tillandsia creates a very warm environment for your home. In most houses, air plants are kept close to the window because of the natural air that they obtain from there. The greatest aspect of this plant is when they are expertly combined with electronics, furniture, carpets and many other home stuff. For instance, you can place your baby Ionantha Rubra or Ionantha Mexican on a coffee table and where the plant is large, you can have them placed in your closet for captivating appearance.

High Survival Chances

One of the things that kill most plants is diseases and pests. Tillandsia has very few pests and diseases that affect them, especially if you take care of them very well. They do not get bugs as other plants do. However, other plants suffer from a host of diseases that easily destroy them. It is as a result of having few natural diseases or pest that air plant has a high rate of survival chances than other plants.

Easy to Care

This is by far one of the unique benefits of having air plants in your home. They require a minimum level of care. They obtain the majority of their nutrients from the air. They do not need any form of soil at all. What they need is a jar, rocks, driftwood and hanging on the wall.

On feeding care, they do not need much amount of food like other plants. They only need fertilizer once in a month. You water them just a couple of times a week except when you live in drier climates where you will need to water them very frequently.

Longevity

Your air plant if well taken care of can live for many years. Air plants are epiphytes meaning that they absorb their nutrients from the air and water compared to other plants that obtain their nutrients from their well-developed roots.

Color Change

This is another unique feature of air plants. They change from one color to another. This is another unique feature of air plants. They change from one color to another. This does not only happen when they are dying, but also as they grow. For instance, Ionantha Fuego is known for growing very well indoors. Tillandsia begins their growth as green, but their leaves will change color the moment they begin to bloom. They have a variety of colors from red, orange, pink, majestic shades of purple and magenta among others.

Exotic Look

Air plants are generally exotic. They come in different amazing shapes and colors. Some have long and thin leaves, while others have shorter leaves yet some have spiky leaves. There are some varieties of air plants that come with beautiful fuzz like texture. However, their exotic look is brought out more when you place them in a container on your desk or even dining table. To add to their exotic look, since air plants do not need any soil for growth, it makes it easier to place them on virtually anything. They can be placed in terrariums, seashell etc.

Minimal Amount of Care

Since watering and fertilizer application is not done every day, you do not have to worry about their excessive care and attention. It means that it is possible to go for a week's vacation and your air plant will still be surviving healthily. They have low maintenance. Some species of air plants in a humid or cooler climate can require water just once a week.

CHAPTER TWO

CLASSIFICATION OF AIR PLANT

Tillandsia Usneoides (Spanish Moss)

This species with a weed-like appearance grows very fast when kept in a greenhouse. It is indigenous to Mexico, Central and South America, United States and the Caribbean. In the

United States, it grows in Texas and Virginia. It has trichome which it uses to trap water for absorption by the plant. The plant is silvery in color.

Care of Tillandsia Usneoides (Spanish Moss)

You can spray it with water. However, spraying is not the most efficient form of watering this air plant. The reason for this is because when you spray the plant with water, the water might only touch the outside only. The best way to water the Spanish moss is to submerge it in water. The plant only needs the normal fertilizer for Tillandsia plants once every month. You can spray the fertilizer on the plant or dunk the plant in the water mixture of your fertilizer.

Tillandsia Cyanea (Pink Quil Plant)

This plant has long slender leaves. When it blooms, it brings forth some sort of purple color flower. The plant does not bloom so easily, so you can order for one from the store or greenhouse garden near you that has the bloom that you want. This plant loves warmer climates.

Care of Tillandsia Cyanea

This plant needs indirect sunlight. If you live in dry climate, you can place your plant in the bathroom so that it can get enough moisture or near your kitchen sink. For watering, this particular species s of plant needs water twice a week. If you live in a humid climate, misting the plant is also very effective. For fertilizer, use a fertilizer that is in a liquid form that has nitrogen and potassium. But let it not contain any form of minerals at all such as copper, boron or iron.

Tillandsia Ionantha

This particular type of plant is inarguably one of the most commercialized and popularly purchased species of air plant. It has different varieties such as Ionantha Guatemala, Mexico, and others. The species of the plant is known to grow very fast within the shortest time and forms a ball during the period of its growth. They are seen mostly in gift shops often. They can also be purchased online. When they are purchased online, they are mostly 2 inches in size, but they will increase in length of growth once they mature. This type of Tillandsia has a lot of species s such as – Ionantha Rubra, Ionantha Scoposa, Mexican, and Fuego etc.

Ionantha Rubra

This species, known for its greenish color is very small in size and the leaves are stiffer and shorter. It grows in a very compact and bulb manner like a garlic. The leaves of this plant are very dense and tender. They are very delicate. It begins its growth with shades of green, red and yellow color depending on the time that the plant enters its bloom phase. One thing with this plant is that as it grows, it will mature and when it does that it will make its own pups. The length of this plant does not go beyond 4 inches. As a result of the small size of this species of plant, it will fit perfectly into cork bark, driftwood, and seashells. They have a lesser amount of trichome for the absorption of nutrients.

Care of Ionantha Rubra

This particular type is known for its low maintenance. This plant thrives well on misting and at least once or twice a week bath by putting the plant under a stream of running water. When watering Ionantha Rubra, it best to place it under a running water because of the bulb that they have. If they are allowed to be immersed or dunk in water, they are more difficult to dry because of the bulb. If your Rubra does not dry, it might rot.

Ionantha Scoposa

This species of plant resembles garlic in appearance. It grows in a compact form and curves as it grows. This plant is mostly found in Guatemala. This plant is among the largest in size within the Ionantha family.

Care of Ionantha Scoposa

This plant does very well in cooler temperatures. It needs more water than other types of Ionantha. Water your plant two to three times in a week. However, because of the bulb which this plant has, never immerse it in water. Water it by placing it under a stream of running water. If you submerge it in water, chances are that the plant might not dry well which will lead to rot.

Ionantha Mexican

This particular type of plant is unique in many respect. It does not rot so easily. When it is time to bloom, it turns bright red before it brings out its purple or green or yellow bloom colors. This plant is mostly found in Mexico and Central America. The plant can also grow on sandy beaches. When the plant matures, they can reach about 2 inches tall at which time they produce pups from their base which can later be separated from the parent plant.

Care of Ionantha Mexican

The easy care of this plant makes it acceptable to many homes. Watering is simple. Just give the plant a weekly bath of two times in a week in a warm water for about forty minutes.

Ionantha Guatemala

This species of plant gotten from the plateau of Guatemala has slender and stiff leaves which are mostly spiky in appearance. The plant is known for its beauty. When the plant reaches maturity they bloom and produce bright purple color. Before the plant reaches maturity, it is normally green in color. The purple and red color only start to appear when the plant begins it bloom circle. One unique feature of this Ionantha species is its rich hue. The plant is used to warm and mild climate in the wild.

Care of Ionantha Guatemala

This plant is very easy to maintain and care for. It requires a bath twice a week. This particular air plant thrives well under indirect sunlight which must be bright. When this particular species of Ionantha is in the blooming phase, never submerge the plant in water. It is best if you place it under a stream of running water and let the water run over it. After watering this species of air plant, the leaves become stiffer when touched. You can use Bromeliad fertilizer on this plant just once in a month. However, if you want faster bloom and growth, you can apply the fertilizer twice in a month. Always allow this plant to dry on a towel before putting it back into the terrarium.

Ionantha Fuego

 This particular variety of Tillandsia Ionantha is known for its colorfulness and is native to Mexico, Central America, where the plants are found in abundance. Besides, the plant grows very rapidly and its maintenance is very low. When the plant matures, it produces pups and if the pups are not separate from the parent plant, they will clump into the form of a ball. When the plant begins to bloom, it changes color from red to white, purple and blue. Due to its size, this plant can make a good fit into a lot of containers that will add a special beauty to your home. It grows to the maximum size of 4 inches. One unique feature of this plant is its ability to go through very extreme conditions including sunny weather. If they come in contact with direct sunlight, they turn bright red in color. However, the more sun this particular air plant is exposed to, the more water they will need very often. Lack of sufficient light for this plant will make them look green.

Care of Ionantha Fuego

The care of this plant requires watering by submersion in water at least for 30 minutes. You can make use of bottled water or rain water for the purposes of watering. If you must use tap water, then allow it to vaporize for the period of at least 12 to 24 hours for the chlorine in the water to be destroyed. If not, they will affect the plant. After watering, place this plant where it will receive a lot of air for it to dry because if it retains water, it will rot.

Tillandsia Xerographica

This species of Tillandsia is normally colorful especially when it is exposed to indirect sunlight. It is one of the commonest species s of air plants. They grow to a very large size when compared to other types of air plants. This plant has the capacity to accommodate high temperature. It has curly silvery leaves and as it grows, the leaves wrap itself around the plant. This grows large and the radiance of this plant can last for a year. This species combines the features of both Xerographica and Fasciculata. It can also handle direct sunlight.

Care of Xerographica

Watering this plant is one of the greatest care that is needed for its survival. Due to the nature of the plant, it often gets rot as one of its common diseases. Water this plant once every two or three weeks.

Since it does not need so much water, it can also handle misting very well. Always ensure that your plant is very dry after it has been watered. The best way to ensure that this plant dries well is to invert it on a towel after it has been watered. To speed up the drying process, make sure that you shake off the excess water on the plant. It uses the normal fertilizer – Bromeliad which should be used once in a month and diluted with water. Preferably, use ¼ of the quantity stated on the bottle of the fertilizer.

Tillandsia Fasciculata

 Fasciculata means fasciculus which implies that something is growing in the bunch. The plant Originates from Jamaica and it can grow in some few areas only. It is also found in Mexico, Brazil, and Central America amongst others. When the proper environment is created for this variety, it will grow very well and show a great and brilliant display that can reach up to a year. The plant has silvery- leaves. The plant can grow up to 8 inches tall.

Care of Fasciculata

 Never expose this plant to a temperature above 78 to 82 degrees Fahrenheit. When the temperature falls below 53 degrees Fahrenheit, the plant could be stressed. It requires indirect sunlight.

Tillandsia Stricta

This very species of plant is known to grow and develop a form of glow. It is native to Brazil, Argentina, Uruguay, Venezuela, and Trinidad. It was first cultivated in 1982 which is a hybrid of the Tillandsia stricta and Tillandsia recurvifolia. When this particular plant begins to bloom, the leaves of this species s turns into a radiant purple color. When blooming is complete, it shows a white and purple color lasting up to one month. The production of pups with this variety is done only once in two years. However, although blooming for this plant takes this long, it is known among the Tillandsia family as one of the fastest growing species s. The bunch which this plant produces is priced highly. The features of this plant are amazing. It has very short stems and they are normally green and grow in a dense clump. When they mature, they reach the length of 4 inches.

Care of Stricta

When introduced to a new environment, the plant can easily adapt without struggles giving it super survival chances more than other plants within the

Tillandsia family. They require a higher amount of light than other Tillandsia plants. Keep them close to the window within the distance of at least 3 cm. Although they require a higher amount of light, direct sunlight will cause sunburn to the plant. If the source of your light is fluorescent bulbs, then keep the plants within the distance of 35 inches from the bulbs. If you use an artificial bulb, make sure that the plant has just 12 hours per day of the light. Proper air circulation is necessary for this plant's growth with the temperature not exceeding 50 – 90 degrees Fahrenheit. The best source of water for this plant is pond water, rain water and water from the aquarium. To water them, give them a bath once a week and if you are in a humid environment, then do that less frequently. They should be soaked for at least 30 minutes or one hour in the water. Let the plant dry before you put them into the terrarium if you are using one. Their drying time is at least 4 hours. Apply your soluble fertilizer once in a month by mixing it with water to increase the speed of growth and blooming. The temperature outdoor requirement for this plant must not fall below 45 degrees Fahrenheit. If the plant rot because of over watering, make sure that you cut off the rotten sections to avoid spreading to the entire plant.

Tillandsia Seleriana

This Tillandsia is known as one of the largest species s that has a rounded bulb with a large base. It is found mostly in Mexico and Central America. It has large silvery leaves. The unique feature of this type of Tillandsia is that it grows in a slow fashion. The color of this air plant is green but when it begins to bloom, the tips of the greenish leave becomes light in color. This plant grows to about 9 inches tall. It has a lot of trichomes giving it a hairy appearance.

Care of Seleriana

The care of this plant is easy. The best watering method for this plant is to put it under a running water. Since the plant has a bulbous base, let the water run through it. Never soak your plant because if you do, it may not dry well and rot may occur. At intervals, you can also mist the plant with water. Before you do that, make sure you invert the plant. It requires cooler temperatures and watering for about 2 to 3 times per week. For sunlight, it requires bright indirect sunlight or filtered sunlight.

Tillandsia Garderi

For a perfect environment, this plant requires indirect sunlight and a very mild level of humidity in a cold environment. It is found in the regions of South and Central America, it has tender leaves and the leaves are silver in color. When this plant matures its leaves becomes rigid and curly. When it blooms, it flowers is normally red and dark purple.

Care of Garderi

This plant needs light from either a filtered source from a shady condition or dappled sunlight. When light is insufficient for this plant, you will begin to notice that the leave of the plant will turn pale. If this happens, make sure that you expose your plant to sufficient light. For fertilizer, soluble fertilizer is good and give the plant bath in it at least once every month. Water this plant two to three times per week. If you are in a drier climate, you might need to water it more often.

Tillandsia Velutina

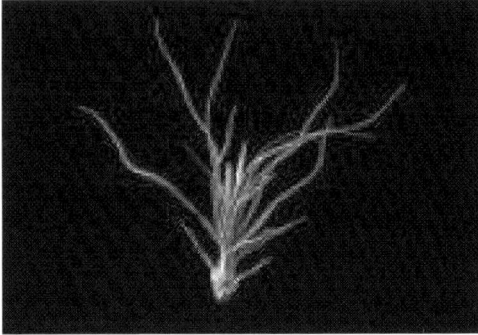

This plant grows in a very compact manner. When it fully matures, it can reach 6 to 8 inches in length. The beauty of this species is unimaginable. It has greenish and tender leaves that arc in a wide manner from its base. The plant thrives highly with indirect light. The maturity of this plant is evidenced by wonderful shades of pink and yellow leaves.

Care of Velutina

The greatest ways to care for this brand of plant is to immerse it in water and then you allow the water to slowly drain from the base. This plant does not need direct sunlight. During winter, put the plant in a bright place. This plant thrives in the normal temperatures for other Tillandsia plants of 50 -90 degrees Fahrenheit.

Tillandsia Pseudobaileyi

Typically found in El Salvador, Guatemala, Mexico, Nicaragua and Honduras, this plant is known for growing very high on trees in the wild. The greatest advantage of this particular type of plant is its adaptability to different environment. This species has many unique features which can be seen in its slender leaves. The color of the leave are silver green and at the edges of the plant, there are normally maroon colored lines that look similar to the ones on onions. During the blooming phase of this species, the plant radiates with maroon color and with time, it produces purple flowers which last for weeks and in some cases up to months. When the bloom dies, pups are produced which remains attached to the plant forming a nice cluster. The pup can be removed once it is one-third of the size of the mother plant.

Care of Pseudobaileyi

 For light, a filtered light of 12 hours per day will be sufficient for this plant. For watering, soak the plant in water once or twice monthly where you live in a humid condition. Allow your Tillandsia to dry entirely by inverting your plant. In a drier climate, soak your plant in water two to three times weekly. Use fertilizer on your plant very sparingly which should be once in a month as recommended in this book. If you want to increase the rate of growth and blooming, then you may have to fertilize two times monthly. For outdoor requirement, do not let the temperature for this plant fall below 50 degrees Fahrenheit.

Tillandsia Tenuifolia

This species of air plant, known for its thick and bushy nature with stiff and strong leaves is native to Central America and South America. When the plant begins to reach maturity, it becomes curvy. Again as the plant grows more and becomes older, its grassy green leaves come from its base and changes to a beautiful bronze color.

When the plant reaches the blooming phase, it brings forth pink and royal blue colored flowers that serve as a serious attraction for pollinators. When matured, the plant can grow to the full height of 5 – 7 inches.

Care of Tenuifolia

Water this plant two to three times per week if you live in dry temperature. The plant loves indirect sunlight. During winter, if your plant is outdoor, remove your plant from there and bring it inside because a fall in temperature below 53 degrees Fahrenheit will kill your plant. The maximum temperature for this plant should not be above 78 degrees Fahrenheit.

Tillandsia Concolor

This particular air plant with its rigid leaves and bold colors and very great inflorescence displayed in bright yellow colors is indigenous to Mexico and Central America. The plant is known for liking bright light. When exposed to bright light, it will display blush of red color. It can grow up to 6 inches in height alone. When the plant reaches the bloom phase, it produces a flower that is a color combination of red and green.

Care of Concolor

 Water this plant according to the degree of your temperature. The plant can thrive from bright light to direct sunlight. Water this particular plant from two to three times per week. The temperature of 50 – 95 Fahrenheit is ideal for this plant.

Tillandsia Argentea

This plant is known for producing a distinctive bloom that expands to the top of the plant and produces a small thin flower. The color of this plant ranges from gray or green depending on the amount of light that is made available to the plant.

Care of Argentea

This plant dries out quickly so you have to observe the plant to see if signs of dryness are beginning to appear on your plant. When it is dry, the leaves curl and the tips become brown. A frequent water soaking will be good for this plant.

Tillandsia Fuchsii

This plant is commonly found in Jamaica, Mexico, and Cuba, it is slender and pale and it has green-silvery leaves that spread out in all direction. It can grow to the height of 2 to 4 inches. One unique feature of this plant is that as the plant matures, it brings out a slender shoot from the middle that blooms a beautiful flower from the tip. The blooming period for this species s occurs in spring.

Care of Fuchsii

This plant requires watering of about 2 – 3 times per week. If you live in dry temperatures, in addition to soaking, mist your plant every day. The light requirement for this plant is a bright light. Indoor temperature or warm temperature is ideal for this air plant.

Tillandsia Capitata

Found mainly in Honduras, Cuba, and Mexico, Guatemala and parts of Central America, the leaves of this plant grows up in an elongated manner and blush when it begins to bloom. It blooms normally in the spring or beginning of summer. It has other types of plant such as capitat peach, maroon capita and yellow capitata. The plant has sword-like leaves. For effective care of this plant, you must expose it to sufficient moisture and indirect light.

Care of Capitata

Water this plant for at least two to three times per week. The best source of water for this plant is lake water, stream, and pond. After watering, allow the plant to dry for at least four hours. To speed up the drying process, make sure that there is enough air for the plant. This plant needs fertilizer for at least once a month mixed with water and the plant is soaked in it.

Tillandsia Bergeri

This plant is native to Argentina where it normally grows on sloppy rocks. Usually, with a unique stalk and flower, this plant is known for its ability to grow very fast. It also produces off shot throughout the year. When the plant matures, it creates dense leaves and the pups begin to emerge from the old mother plant. When it blooms, it produces a pale pink flower with violet petals.

Care of Tillandsia Bergeri

Water this plant 2- 3 times per week and allow it to dry after watering with enough air circulation. The best water for this plant is pond water, rainwater, etc.

Tillandsia Aeranthos

With stiff and sharp leaves, this plant grows up from the center. It is indigenous to Central America. The slender leaves blush as the plant approaches maturity. During the blooming phase of the plant, it produces a lovely flower in purple, blue and pink which can last for many weeks. Due to its colorful bloom, there are many hybrid types of this variety. It is commercially productive. The shape of this plant gives you the flexibility to use it for multiple designs in your home and in your porch.

Care of Aeranthos

The best temperature for this plant is between the ranges of 57 to 82 degrees Fahrenheit. It requires indirect sunlight. Water this plant 2- 3 times per week and allow it to dry after watering with enough air circulation. The best water for this plant is pond water, rainwater among others.

Tillandsia Xeric

These are air plants that can survive in dry climates. To survive, they have a lot of trichomes which helps them to effectively use the small amount of moisture that is available. They do not need so much watering and they can survive under direct sunlight. Their leaves are silver in color.

Care of Tillandsia Xeric

The general care that has been stated under the topic Air Plant Care and Maintenance will be enough for this type of Tillandsia.

Tillandsia Mesic

Unlike their other cousins, the Mesic Tillandsia species s require medium moisture. They are mostly found in South American forests and these plants require moderate humidity and regular watering. They do not have many trichomes and their leaves are dark green in color. Indirect sunlight is the best for them. In the wild, the shades that trees provide serves as a medium that the direct sunlight for the plant is reduced. If the sunlight becomes too much, they may be burnt by it and they can eventually die off.

Tillandsia Juncea

With its royal purple color and grass-like appearance, Tillandsia Juncea has a slow growth rate. The plant has a brown base. Before this plant begins to bloom, a thin bloom of spiky nature will appear on the plant.

<u>Care of Juncea</u>

This plant requires watering of about 2-3 times weekly. If not properly watered, this plant tends to die out. This Tillandsia also requires bright light. Temperature requirement of 50-90 Fahrenheit is ideal. This plant is adapted to outdoor life. Grows up in clump and reaches 6 – 8 inches.

Air Plants Growth Phases

Air plants have different phases of development. Below are the phases of their development.

Blooming Phase

This is a unique time in the life of
Tillandsia. Being tropical plants that live
for many years, they bloom only once in
the period of their entire existence. The
type of flowers that they will produce
during the blooming phase of their
development depends on the particular
species of air plant. Their flowers are

generally brighter in color and the blooming phase usually last for many days or months, depending on the species of air plant that you have. One thing though influences the blooming of your plant – the care and the environment of your air plant. That is why you have to create the perfect environment for your air plant to encourage them to bloom. Some air plant bloom in the middle of winter or summer.

Making Air Plant Bloom Fast

If you want to see your air plant bloom quickly, then buy plants that have already started growing pups. Make sure that you adhere strictly to the care of the plant. Apply fertilizers such as orchid or Bromeliad once in a month by soaking them in the fertilizer mixed with water in order to speed up the process of blooming. Again, it is good to know the life cycle of an air plant before you order it. Knowing the life cycle of your air plant will help you to determine the bloom time of that particular species. If you want to speed up blooming, then you must care for your plant.

Pups Phase

When your air plant begins to bloom, they produce pups (baby air plants) that come from the mother plant as offshoots. This only happens when Tillandsia reaches the advanced stage of growth. The pups usually have a form of different center that makes it easy to distinguish them from the leaves of the plant. Whenever the pups reached at least one-third or two-third of the size of the mother plant, they can be separated. The pup is removed by gently pulling and twisting it carefully from the mother plant. To remove it, hold the mother plant and the pup. Gently, twist the pup to separate it from the mother plant. You can employ the use of razor blades for the purpose of separating the plant from the mother. This pup which you now hold in your hands will grow following different phases of development, becoming a mother plant, blooming and one day produce its own pup before it dies off.

If the Tillandsia species that you have produces many offshoots you can leave them alone, they will eventually grow into an attractive spherical clump. Where Tillandsia are pollinated, they produce seeds that look like dandelion seedlings that can be germinated. Tillandsia seedlings grow very slowly and they can take many years that is why many people prefer it pupping by producing its babies.

You may desire to grow your pups different from the mother plant. If that is what you want, then there may be a need for you to remove the pups and put them some else where they can grow. You need a sharp knife or blade. Cut the air plant from the base of the parent carefully. Do not make the mistake of cutting more or less from the mother. You cut less, you might damage the parent or mother plant. When these plants are separated, they can grow into full size and make their own baby Tillandsia.

Clumping Phase

This is another phase of air plant development. When the Tillandsia pups are not removed from the mother plant, they will grow into clumps. The clump can also be created by connecting many plants together using a wire. As that is done, the plant grows around one another.

Choosing Air Plant

The first question is, what type of plant should I take if I live in New York or Chicago or even Texas? Or for a person who lives in places where the climate is dry? If you live in a dry climate then certain types of Tillandsia will be better off for you. If you live in drier places of the united States such as Florida, Arizona, Texas, South Carolina or in drier places of the United Kingdom like Essex, Cambridgeshire or in Canada places like Kelonowa, then the best species of air plant will be the silvery xeric species as it does not require too much watering than other members of the same family. Again, the place where you display your Tillandsia is of equally great importance since there are some plants that need a lot of light than others. Some of the important things to consider before choosing your Tillandsia are discussed below.

Environment

This will have a lot of impact on the type of Tillandsia that you can grow. As said earlier, there are some species of air plants that require a lesser amount of water. There are some that have mastered the art of living in a dry climate while others prefer humid weather or climates. It is important to know that the level of humidity or moisture can affect the growth rate of your plant. Most air plants slow down their growth rate during winter. This will also affect the time that they bloom.

Light

Most varieties of air plants, use indirect light. There are however some air plants that accept direct sunlight and still do very well in them. These are things to be taken into consideration whenever you are deciding on what air plant to choose from.

Air

Silver-colored Tillandsia gets their nutrients from the air. So if they are in containers such as terrariums or other types of containers, make sure that they are left open. Do not shut down the cover or vent through which air passes to your plant. If you do that, the plants will suffer from lack of nutrients and they will eventually die off. This is another thing to be considered when choosing air plants. There must be sufficient air circulation for this plant if they must grow well and bloom. This is another major factor that you will take into consideration when choosing your air plant.

Moisture

Humidity and moisture will definitely affect the care that you will give to your plant. Even the watering of your plant will be affected by moisture. The more humidity, the less you will water your air plant. If you want to water your air plant less frequently or you are someone who travels a lot, then this will affect the Tillandsia that you will choose.

Air Plant Shopping

Shopping for an air plant is something that is cool and exciting provided that you are armed with certain information. There are several places where you can buy your air plant. You can get them from the greenhouse that is located nearby. However, before you make purchases on amazon or any retailers that sell Tillandsia you will want to make sure that you read all the reviews about their services. Read all reviews for the Tillandsia and including the negative ones. You can order them from there. However, you can make purchases online from retail stores that sell plants. Some stores offer you free Tillandsia tips for your air plant once you make your purchases from them. They will offer you some tips on how to take care of your plant, how to put your plant in a terrarium, applying fertilizer to your air plant and some basic tips. They will give you a head start on what you need to do for your air plant to grow and bloom.

In addition, before you shop for your air plant, you need to know that you want. Do you want a plant that will bloom within a few weeks after you order them, then you may have to consider buying mature Tillandsia that is almost ready to bloom. Do you want to watch and see your air plant grow, then you may consider buying pups and taking good care of them until they have reached maturity and are ready to bloom and make their own babies or pups. When making your purchases online, sort your preference by type or species and then price. Since you already knew what you want. When you have done all these things, then you can order for your air plant.

What Next After Your Air Plant Arrived

Due to the shipping of your plant, the plant might be stressed. The first thing to do after the plant has been shipped to you to reduce the stressed that the plant has gone through, you have to, first of all, soak them in water, a bath for approximately 20-30 minutes. When it comes to their first bath in a new environment, do not just bath them with any kind of water. Use a lukewarm water for your plant. Allow the plant to dry completely. If the plants have roots make sure that you cut them off. Give your new plant sufficient light source for both outdoor and indoor requirements. Do not apply fertilizer to your plant

within three weeks after they have been
shipped to you.

CHAPTER THREE

PERFECT AIR PLANT ENVIRONMENT

Air quality

To survive and bloom very well, air plant needs a good air circulation and quality.

The following points are discussed under air quality.

Humidity

Most of the air plants thrive well with a medium level of humidity and when the atmosphere is dry, some of them cannot thrive. However, where the plants are in dry areas, they can survive by frequent immersion in water in order to compliment the dryness in the atmosphere. The good thing about this plant is that if they are kept in good humid conditions, they need less watering and immersion in water.

Air Circulation

The good circulation of air is necessary for the survival of plants. This becomes important when the plants are watered because they will need air so that they can dry within four hours. If you are using any form of container for the display of your air plant, you must make sure that you do not close it up so that the plant can have enough air that will circulate for effective growth. This also helps because if the lid of the container is closed, moisture will be trapped inside causing a lot of harm to your plant.

Temperature

Air plant needs a good temperature which must be between 50 to 90 degrees Fahrenheit. However, when you read through the different species of air plants in this book, you will notice that the plants have different requirement for temperature. While some species of Tillandsia require a temperature of 78 degrees Fahrenheit, others can take higher temperatures. A thermometer will help in knowing the precise temperature within your environment. Being plants that are used to life in the tropics, they should be placed in areas where the temperature can ensure their survival. Again, extreme cold can do more harm to your plant. If you keep your Tillandsia close to the window, always ensure that you create some level of distance from your plant. While these plants have a good adapting ability to changing environmental conditions, if this is too sudden, it can cause severe shock to the plant and they may die off.

Light

Tillandsia needs a light that is bright. However, they can be left in direct sunlight. However, when you place your air plant under direct sunlight for some hours, they must be misted regularly in a week so that they can be kept hydrated. During summer, however, it is not advisable to leave your plant under the power of the scorching sun. If you do that, it is likely that your plant will become sunburnt. Where the plant is kept close to the window, then it is necessary that the plant is kept within the distance of 3 feet from the bright light that is coming from the window.

Artificial Light

Although an air plant should be kept under the indirect light, however, they can also do well under indirect light. They can be kept under fluorescent light in the home or office. Fluorescent light is regarded as the best light for air plant once the plant is to make use of artificial light. The plant can be as close to the fluorescent light within the range of 6 inches while a distance of 36 inches is great for your plant. If they are too close, the heat from the fluorescence tube might cause them to be burnt or where they are too close, it will dry them of their moisture.

Water

Watering your air plant should be done in the morning and should be done at least two to three times per week, depending on the type of environment that you live in. For those in drier climates, they will need to water their plants more than those in a humid climate. Once you have watered your plant, one thing that you want to ensure is that you create enough air circulation for the plant with sufficient light to go with. This is so that your plant will have the perfect condition to dry. The drying process might take up to four hours. Misting your air plant will be greatly inadequate, especially for those who live in a dry climate. However, you can mist your air plant as a means of complimenting the overall watering of your plant.

CHAPTER FOUR

Air Plant Feeding

Your plant needs proper feeding care to grow and bloom.

Water

Regularly watering your air plant will enhance their growth and development.

Best Water for Your Air Plant

Air plant are not normally selective on the type of water they need. However, there are certain types of water that are best suited for your plant such as - pond water, rainwater, water from the aquarium, etc. Although you can use tap water to water your air plants, if you are not careful, they can damage your air plant because of the presence of chlorine in the water. If you want to use tap water after collecting it from the tap, do not use it immediately to water your plant. Since the best time to water air plant is in the morning, it is good for you to collect your tap water and keep it for the period of 12 to 24 hours so that it can evaporate before you use it to water your plant. Keeping your plant for such a long time will kill the chlorine content of tap water. It is also possible to make use of water from the spring or bottled water. If your water contains any form of salt, it can damage your plant. Do not use softened water because of its high salt content. If you do, it can destroy your plant. If the water in your area is hard water, then do not use it on your air plant. The chalk content of the hard water will clog the trichome of the air plant.

Methods of Watering Air Plant

There are several ways by which you can water your air plant. Let us consider some of them.

The Drenching Method

Watering air plant by this method can be done once in a week depending on the type of environment that the plant is. While those in a drier climate will be required to water their plants more often, those in a humid climate will be required to water their plant lesser. Generally, air plants can be drenched for at least 15 minutes. Once the plant is soaked, you can shake off the remaining water from the plant and it leaves. If you allow the water to remain on the leave, damage can be done to your air plant in the form of rot. The moment you are done with drenching the plant, gently place the plant upside down on a towel for the excess water to drain away. You can also put the plant in a place with good air circulation for effective drying.

Immersion Method

Immerse your plant in the water as many times as possible, then carefully shake off the excess water. It all depends on your environment, it takes about four hours for the plant to dry completely.

Vaporization Method

This is another method of watering your air plant. Some plants like vapor while others do not. For plants that like vapor especially those that require a very little quantity of water, vapor can be used. When the weather is dry, the use of vapor can stop dryness of the tips of your plant leaves.

Blooming Phase Watering

That is one of the beautiful moment of the life of an air plant. When it begins to bloom in exciting and energetic colors of purple, pink, yellow, depending on the type that you have. When you want to water your plant during the blooming phase, special care must be taken. Never immerse the flower that has bloomed in water. If you do this, your flower will rot within the shortest time. You water the plant during the blooming phase by putting the plant under running water so that it will wet. Never water the blooming flower, else it will be damaged.

The Best Time to Water Air Plant

The best time to water your plant is in the morning. Most species of air plants normally absorb their nutrients using their leaves in the early evening hours. While carbon dioxide is taken at night. If the leaves are wet it will hinder them from absorbing essential nutrients for their growth. If you soak your plant in the water during the morning hours, the plant will dry before evening, which is the time they take in nutrients.

Fertilizer

Your Tillandsia needs some level of fertilizer to grow well and bloom in beautiful colors within the required time. This becomes necessary when they are about to pup. The fertilizer helps the plant to pup very well. The fertilizer offers the plants some of the essential nutrients which they need. A fertilizer with a lower level of nitrogen, when used carefully and infrequently, can have a lot of effects on your plants. It will influence their growth, pups, and aids their bloom phase and cycles. In the market today, there are several fertilizers that can be applied to Tillandsia plants but diluted orchid or bromeliad fertilizer are good for your plants. When using fertilizer for your plants, make sure the one that you are using is a non-urea nitrogen fertilizer. Urea based fertilizers can only be broken down by plants that have that have roots. They are able to absorb nutrients because of the bacterial presence in the soil. Unfortunately for air plants, they do not have the capacity to use this kind of nitrogen in the soil because they do not take their nutrients using roots but leaves. If you use this type of fertilizer for your plant, it will destroy your plant.

NPK fertilizers are explained by the quality of nitrogen, potassium, and phosphorus clearly stated. For survival, your Tillandsia plant needs all these three factors that were stated above. The benefits of nitrogen to plants are numerous – ensure that their new leaf grows, repairing of tissues, and ensure that the leaves grow longer. The flowering of your plant will be enhanced by phosphorus while potassium is important for the growth of your plant. When you use fertilizer excessively, it can damage your plant. Tillandsia has a high level of sensitivity to fertilizer. For good results, it is suggested to dilute the fertilizer in water and then immerse the plant in it once every month. If you buy your fertilizer in a bottle, I will recommend that you put a third or fourth of what the bottle says you should do. If the bottle says a tablespoon for a gallon, then apply a third of a tablespoon. Use fertilizer on your plant sparingly and always watch to see their response to the fertilizer.

Care and Maintenance of Air Plant

The common believe that many people have is that since air plants are epiphyte, they do not need maintenance. Contrary to that belief, your air plant still needs low maintenance.

Tillandsia Indoor and Outdoor Care

The requirement for the care and maintenance of your Tillandsia varies. If the plants are indoors, it will require a different kind of care. The same thing happens if your plants are outdoors. You will need a different kind of maintenance for your plant.

Light

The light requirement for your air plant should be bright but indirect light. Though this depends on the species because there are some varieties of air plant that can thrive well with direct sunlight. Tillandsia can be grown in the house and placed close to the window. However, let it not be too close to the window because if the light is too much, it can get your plant sunburnt. When it is summer time, move your plant away from the window to avoid a situation where too much heat might destroy your plant. However, when it is winter time, bring it closer to the window so that it can get all the light that it can get from the sun for the effective growth of your plant. If you have trees close to your window, you may consider creating enough passage for filtered light so that your plant is not starved of light for photosynthesis. You can also use artificial light such as fluorescent bulbs for your plant. Set your light with a timer. The maximum should not be more than 12 hours in a day. If you are using artificial light, never place your plant too close to heat generating bulbs, it will damage your plant.

Water

Depending on the species of the plant that you have, it is required to water air plant at least two to three times per week. There are however some species that need less water than others. Never rely on spraying mist on your plant as the sole form of watering your Tillandsia. It will not be enough for your plant and dehydration can occur. The only time you can spray mist is to use it in addition to watering your Tillandsia. Your air plant takes up water through their trichome which is a wooly and white substance on the plant. The Trichome opens up once water touches them and then they trap the water so that the plant can absorb it. Soaking your plant in water is one of the ways to give your plant enough water for their survival and avoid dehydration. If you mount your plant on something like a driftwood, make sure that it is something that can be wet. If the plants are large, then you may need a bigger watering bowl for your plant. When you bath your plant, shake off excess water, either you put your Tillandsia to lie by the side or vertically. Depending on your species, you may turn your plant upside down so that it can dry.

Air

Your indoor air is very important for your Tillandsia. After you water your plant, you have to allow them to dry for a long time. The reason why air circulation is important is because the plant takes up their nutrients from the air too.

The normal room temperature is ideal for your plant. However, Tillandsia generally requires a temperature between the ranges of 50 – 90 degrees Fahrenheit.

Outdoor Care

<u>Light</u>

Light for your Tillandsia in outdoor condition should be a bright light but supplied through filtered medium. When you place your plant outdoors, then a pool enclosure or screen porch gives them the light that they need. Filtered light which comes directly from larger trees is ideal for your plant since they form small spots of dotted light. Dappled light can also be used for your plant and they will grow under it. The difference between filtered light and dappled light is their size. Dappled light looks bigger underneath a tree, but filtered light is smaller. Dapple light stays constant throughout the day until the time when the sun begins to set. They are ideal for your outdoor Tillandsia plant. You can also decide to give your plant a direct sunlight for a little time in the morning while you watch them carefully.

Water

 For our outdoor plants, wet them at least two to three times per week. When they are in a hot climate, especially as they are outside, they will need a more frequent bath. When they have their bath, ensure that you give them sufficient air and light for them to dry effectively. They actually need about 4 hours to dry on a towel. If you keep your Tillandsia in water, it is possible that they will rot. When they are under watered, the leaves will look curvy.

Temperature

The normal and required temperature for Tillandsia is 50-90 degrees Fahrenheit. When they are outside and the temperature rises above 90 degrees Fahrenheit or falls below 50 degrees Fahrenheit, then you may need to take your plant indoors. The high temperature will stress them and dehydration will result. If the plants are stressed by high temperature, they can be damaged. During winter, it is recommended to bring your plant indoors because Tillandsia is allergic to too much cold. If the temperature falls below 35 degrees Fahrenheit, frost will cause severe damage to your plant.

Reviving a Dying or Sick Air Plant

When an air plant is sick or dying, is there anything that can be done to revive the plant?

While misting air plant with water can work for some species, in other varieties, this will not work. It will ultimately lead to their dead.

The first thing to do for a sick or dying air plant is to bath the plant or soak it in water overnight. Then in the morning, remove the plant from the water. Shake it off and install the plant back to its place. Remove all the dead leaves from your plant. If while doing this, you noticed that the whole plant falls apart, then your plant is dead. However, where it is just a few leaves that fell off and other ones are greenish and healthy-looking, then your plant is still alive. Where it is the tip of the plants that are turning brown, then your solution lies in an overnight bath for your plant. After the first therapy, then water them more often and do it regularly. Sometimes because of leaving your plant in a water for too long, you will notice that the plant falls off even if they are still green. Make sure that when watering your air plant, you do that by giving them a bath of thirty minutes to one hour and no more. If you allow them in the water for too long, then that will cause this particular problem of the leaves falling off even when they look green. Make sure that you dry the air plant by laying them down on a towel normally in an upside down position for about 4 hours for them to dry well.

Another way to revive a dying or sick air plant is to soak your plant in a container and take it indoor to a room with a temperature of about 66 to 75 degrees Fahrenheit. Set the container in a spot where it can receive bright and indirect sunlight on any surface that is flat. Let the air plant soak in the container for approximately 12 hours. Take out the plant from water, then shake off excess water. After you do that, dry it for about four hours. Allow your air plant to dry. Make sure that you keep an eye on your plant if you can see signs of the leaf curling within the period of two or three days after you had bathed them in water. If the leaves are curly, then you will submerge the air plant in water and allow it for the period of four hours. Shake off excess water carefully and dry it. In an empty bowl, pour water of about 70% and Isopropyl. Get your pruning shares and dunk them in water solution for about 5 minutes. After removing the blade and rinsing them, use them to cut off your Tillandsia leaves that looked dead.

CHAPTER FIVE

Displaying and Mounting Air Plant

There are a lot of objects that air plants can be mounted on. Cork bark, driftwood, seashells among others. A waterproof glue such as E 6000 can be used to attach your Tillandsia to display objects. When applying your glue, apply the adhesive from the base of the plants at the center so that it does not stop the roots from growing up. You can use silver wire to hold the glue temporarily until when it is firm. If you are using terrarium, then use a light fishing gauge till the roots of the plant bed attach to the terrarium. Do not use copper wire because the copper in the wire is toxic to the plants.

Terrarium

When you desire to display your air plants, one of the first display media that you will consider is a terrarium. This is because they are very easy to install. Again terrarium can be changed without any form of problem. There are two types of terrarium that you will find them in many places - hanging terrarium or terrarium with a flat bottom that can be used or placed on tables and on shelves. Depending on taste and choice, you can decide to place your air plant alone in your terrarium or you can decide to add moss, tree bark, sand or stones.

Containers

These containers can be called natural
containers because they are gotten from
the ocean. These are sea urchins,
seashells etc. Many of these containers
have little holes that make air plant to
perfectly fit into them. If the species of
Tillandsia that you have is big, then you
can employ the use of conch shells. Sea

pods and small wood pots can also be used for the purposes of housing your air plant.

Driftwood, Grapevine and Mopani

In the wild, Tillandsia most often attaches themselves to the side of trees, stones, and rocky cliffs. You can use different types of home to offer your plants the feel of their natural habit like they have in the wild. Your driftwood can be used. And your plant can easily attach themselves to the wood by the use of glue like E 6000 waterproof glue. Grape and Mopani woods can be used for the display of your air plant.

Cork Bark

You can display your air plant on cork bark. You can cut the cork bark for easy usage to hang on your wall and table displays.

Gardens

Gardens are good media for the display of your Tillandsia. Many people use the air plant vertical garden for the display of their Tillandsia. It is made up of wire mesh and the Tillandsia are inserted in the openings of the wire mesh.

Bird cage

Your bird cage can be such amazing way to display your Tillandsia. To add some form of beauty to the plant, insert some pieces of wood or branches in the cage and your Tillandsia will feel more at home like they do in the wild.

<u>Baskets</u>

Creativity has no limitation and if you want to enjoy displaying your Tillandsia, then your basket will offer you an option that you will enjoy. When they are growing in a basket, they look beautiful and amazing.

Air Plant on Stones

This is another great way to display your air plant. Since in the wild air plant attaches themselves to stones, you can create just the same home for them by a displaying them on the stone. The art of displaying them on stones is always beautiful to see.

Display on Posts

If you have a slat that is on your patio, then you may consider displaying your

Tillandsia on them. You can tie let say a bundle of air plants to the slat for decorative outlook.

Bowls

It may surprise you to know that your Tillandsia can be displayed in bowls. Any colorful bowl will be sufficient to display your plant.

<u>Wire</u>

You can display your air plant on the wire. All you need to do so to place our air plant around some moss and turn it into any form of shape that you like and then cover it for effective display.

How to Care for Air Plants Displayed in Terrariums

Although larger Tillandsias cannot be displayed in this way and manner, but smaller Tillandsias can be converted into a work of art. Because these plants are in a container, they will require a different amount of care than other air plants.

The first thing you want to ensure that you do is to remove your air plant from the container before you water it. This is because your container carries a different type of humidity. It is hotter than other forms of climate within your environment. Never place your terrarium or display glass close to the window but give some distance away from the window. Your window increases the rays of sunlight that enters your home. If you do that, your plant can be sunburnt. The best glass to use is a large glass because of the smaller the glass, the lesser the amount of air and the larger the glass, the larger the amount of air that will be available for circulation.

How to Care for Mounted Air Plants

One problem with mounted air plants is that you might not be able to soak them in water. As a result of that, these types of plant require a different type of care. In the case of air plant that are in containers, they have higher levels of humidity. Since these plants are mounted, they will require a higher amount of misting. They may need to be watered two times a week. This will enable the plants to stay hydrated.

Air Plants Trimming

As your air plant grows, sometimes you will notice that the leaves of your Tillandsia may need a little trimming.

Whenever you see the leaves of your Tillandsia looking brown, it does not mean that something is wrong with them. They need some trimming. It is possible for the leaves of your plants to come out because of the fact that they are trying to acclimatize themselves to the new environment that you brought them. That may be the reason why they are having dry leaves. You can remove the dry leaves by pulling them. You can also use a scissor to trim it off by cutting it at an angle that will make it look somewhat pointy. This may become necessary where some parts of the leaves are not dry. You can also trim off the roots of the plant. After trimming your plants off, it is important to know that the leaves of the plants will still grow back and regenerate. When the leaves turn brown, your remedy will be to trim it off. It is a natural process that your air plants are experiencing. Most air plants are shipped with their roots complete, but you can trim them off. Remember that the roots are used for one purpose by the plants – to attach the plants to other display media.

While trimming is important as this will help the plant to grow back, you must, however, exercise some caution when doing so. The reason for this is if you are not careful in trimming your plants you may damage the base of the plant when you trim the roots in excess. Use your scissors cautiously. Smaller scissors and sharp knives are the ones that are recommended for perfect trimming. To make it easier for you to cut off the roots of your air plant, you may soak the roots in water for some few minutes before proceeding to trim them off.

For your dry leaves, it is important to trim them off because if left without trimming, the dry leaves can trap a lot of humidity which may stop the plant from drying effectively. The moment this happens, your plant will rot. Besides that, if you trim your plant, Tillandsia looks more beautiful than when they have dry leaves. However, when trimming the leaves of your air plant, you have to make sure that you thoroughly check your plant to see if it has a pup that is growing beneath the leaves. If a pup is growing underneath the leaves and you trim the leave, you may harm the pup. If there is a pup growing under the leave, then it is best to let it alone for a while until the pup reaches one-third of the size of the mother plant before you trim off the leaves. If the leaves of your air plant are broken off, they can also be trimmed. Do it cautiously. Make sure that you do not over cut the other part that is not broken as this may affect their ability to absorb nutrients.

How to Divide Air Plants

One day, a time is coming when you will have to decide on this important subject of diving your air plant. The production of pups will necessitate the dividing your air plant. Diving air plants come immediately after the blooming phase of the plant. Depending on your air plant, blooming may take up to several months or even years. When the mother Tillandsia blooms, then the plant begins to produce pups. They come as an offshoot of the mother. You will still need to keep taking care of the mother plant after it has bloomed. Water the mother plant following the normal watering care stated in this book. You have to be cautious with the pups so you do not damage them because they are delicate when they are growing up.

Your task of dividing the pups from the parent plant comes when the pups reach one-third of the mother plant. There are two methods of dividing your air plant.

Hand method

 You can use your hand to divide the pups from the mother plant. Using your hands, hold the parent plant at their bases and carefully turn your hands down.

Cutting Method

This is another method of diving air plants. If you want to do a clean job, then you may have to use a sharp knife or garden shears. You should cut the pups by using your scissor as close to the mother plant as you can be. Once you are done with trimming your pups, do not put back the plant into your terrarium or container yet. Allow both the parent plant and the pup to have their separation point restored back and hardened. Leave both mother and plant to dry off before putting them back into the container. It will prevent bacterial growth at the place of the cutting.

CHAPTER SIX

Air Plant Pest and Diseases

The best thing about air plant is that they have the ability to resist pests and diseases. Even where these diseases begin to trouble your plant, the treatment is simple to administer to your plant. The pests which normally attack air plants are scales like Mealy bugs and Aphids.

The treatment is simple. All you need to do is simply to spray the bugs out of the plant with ordinary water. You can also make use of a nontoxic solution of dish soap. You can rub alcohol on the plant. Where the pest has severely attacked the plant, the most effective way to treat it is to mix baby shampoo in water and cover the entire plant in it. Allow it to soak like that for a few minutes, then make sure that you rinse the plant very well from the soup. However, if all efforts to do away with the pest fails, then you may consider the use of an insecticide at this point.

Scale

Scale insects are very small insects that form a waxy wall that gives them protection as they suck the sap of the plant. Types of scale insects.

Mealy bugs

Mealy bugs suck the sap of plant and they produce a waxy cotton like materials that serves as protection from predators. Once you noticed that a white cotton like material covers your air plant, then it is mealy bug that is attacking your plant. For effective treatment, you have to first separate the plant from other air plants. After doing that, then you have to use a dish soap on your plant. Either you make use of cotton swabs for dabbing the leaves or you spray the soap on the plant after diluting it. The dish soap works in a great way by suffocating the pests through the barriers it creates on the plant. Thus, after the pest has been dealt with, you have to ensure that you properly rinse the plant from all the soap else, it will suffocate the plant.

Aphids

Aphids also suck the sap of air plant, however, the harm that they cause is normally small. It is very uncommon to find Aphids that do a lot of damage to

Tillandsia. You can locate aphids by checking under the base of your leaves because that is where they love to hide. The treatment for aphids is pretty easy. You can use your hands and hit them off your plant. If that does not work, then you can remove them by using your soap spray. Once you do that, make sure that you properly clean the soap from the plant.

Rot

This is another common disease of air plant. Although air plant needs good humidity to grow and bloom effectively, when it is exposed to too much moisture, the death of the plant can occur. The plant will simply rot from the inside and then fall away. The common ways to know that your air plant is suffering from too much humidity or moisture is your plant becoming black or developing a tender base, and it begins to fall off or the inside looks soft and black, or it shows the growth of mold. When this occurs, it is a clear sign that your plant is being damaged by rot.

Rot is caused by allowing water to stay in the leaves of your air plant. It is also caused keeping the Tillandsia moistened or keeping your plant in an environment where it is not allowed to dry very well. To prevent rot, especially for indoor Tillandsia plants, before you water your plant, make sure that you remove it from the shell, or case or terrarium. Once you have watered your air plant, then you place it in an environment that allows it to dry fully before bringing it back to the shell or Terrarium or whatever vessel that you are using to display your plant. When you water your plant in the shell or container, the moisture that stays in the container can cause the plant to rot. When your plant gets too wet, shake the water off it. You can also employ the use of a fan to speed up the process of drying or put your plant in a place where there is good air circulation. Most rot in Tillandsia plants will eventually lead to the death of the plant. So avoid too much moisture for your plants.

<u>Mildew</u>

The Tillandsia Xerographica suffers most from this particular fungi attack. This mildew normally appears on this air plant when the plant is too wet and has not been allowed to dry well. It starts as whitish powdery spots on your Xerographica leaves and sometimes it turns yellowish brown. If you noticed that there are white powdery spots on your plant and the Tillandsia leaf begins to fall off, then your plant is suffering from mildew. Always ensure that your plant is dry before you take them indoors. Ensure that your plant is exposed to sunlight directly or indirectly to ward off this particular pest. Since the main plant that suffers from these diseases is the Xcrographica which can take in direct sunlight, you can expose the plant to direct sunlight or keep it close to the window so that the plant can get enough indirect sunlight. Good air circulation will also eliminate this disease from your plant. If you noticed this, then make sure that your plant has enough air circulation. If the plant has clumped, then you may consider dividing the pups from the parent plant for good air circulation to take place.

Exposure to too Much Sunlight

For your air plant to grow and bloom, one necessary requirement is indirect light. However, where the light is direct, it will likely destroy the plant. When you begin to notice that the tip of your plant is becoming brown in color or yellow spots appearing on it, then it is a clear case that your plant is being destroyed by exposure to direct sunlight. Although some species of air plants can do very well in sunlight, if they are in direct sunlight then you must water them very often. However, the majority of the types of Tillandsia does well in shades where they receive indirect sunlight.

Cold Weather

When the weather is cold, Tillandsia can be greatly affected. When you begin to notice that your plant turns black or brown in color, then the cold or frozen weather is affecting it. Although some species of air plant can survive cold weather than other types, however an air plant that is affected by cold may die. Prevention is your best solution.

Dehydration

This is one of the common problems of Tillandsia. Depending on the species, the minimum number of times that you can water Tillandsia is once a week. If you do not water your air plant as you should, it is possible for your plant to be dehydrated. To avoid dehydration, make sure that you water your air plant two to three times in a week. If you notice signs of dehydration from your plant, immediately hydrate them so that they do not die because of lack of water.

CHAPTER SEVEN

Air Plant Gardening Tools

Watering Bowl

Prunning Shears

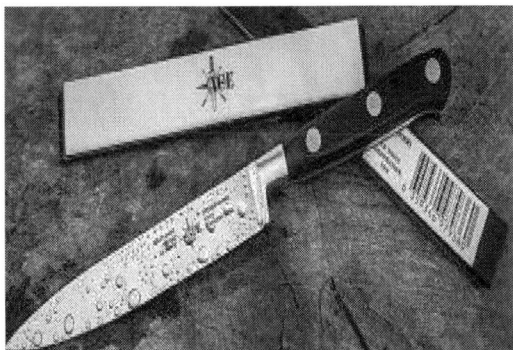

Sharp Knife

Printed in Great Britain
by Amazon